Teach Me...™
Everyday
SPANISH
Volume 1

Written by Judy Mahoney
Illustrated by Patrick Girouard

Technology is changing our world. Far away exotic places have literally become neighbors. We belong to a global community and our children are becoming "global kids." Comparing and understanding different languages and cultures is more vital than ever! Additionally, learning a foreign language reinforces a child's overall education. Early childhood is the optimal time for children to learn a second language, and the Teach Me Everyday language series is a practical and inspiring way to teach them. Through story and song, each book and audio encourages them to listen, speak, read and write in a foreign language.

Today's "global kids" hold tomorrow's world in their hands. So when it comes to learning a new language, don't be surprised when they say, "teach me!"

The Spanish language consists of two branches: Castilian Spanish, which is spoken in Spain; and American Spanish, which is spoken in most of the countries in Latin America. These forms of Spanish differ just slightly in terms of conjugation forms used, and the pronunciation of some letters. Spanish-speaking countries and regions may have their own dialect or variation of the language and pronunciation.

Teach Me Everyday Spanish
Volume One
ISBN 13: 978-1-59972-102-6
Library of Congress PCN: 2008902653

Copyright © 2008 by Teach Me Tapes, Inc.
6016 Blue Circle Drive, Minnetonka, MN 55343
www.teachmetapes.com

Book Design by Design Lab, Northfield, MN

10 9 8 7 6 5 4 3 2

INDEX & SONG LIST

Lo Más Que Nos Reunimos

Lo más que nos reunimos, reunimos, reunimos
Lo más que nos reunimos, seremos felices
Tus amigos son mis amigos
Y mis amigos son tus amigos
Lo más que nos reunimos, seremos felices.

The More We Get Together
The more we get together, together, together
The more we get together, the happier we'll be
For your friends are my friends
And my friends are your friends
The more we get together, the happier we'll be.

My father
My brother
My mother
Me

Mi gato.
Él se llama Mishu.
Él es de color gris.

My cat.
His name is Mishu.
He is the color gray.

mi gato

This is my house.
My house has a red
roof and a garden
with yellow flowers.

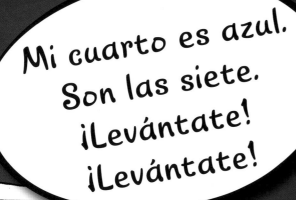

My room is blue.
It is seven o'clock.
Get up!
Get up!

Fray Felipe

Fray Felipe, Fray Felipe
¿Duermes tú? ¿Duermes tú?
Suenan las campanas
Suenan las campanas.
¡Din Dan Don!
¡Din Dan Don!

Are You Sleeping

Are you sleeping, are you sleeping
Brother John? Brother John?
Morning bells are ringing
Morning bells are ringing.
Ding Dang Dong!
Ding Dang Dong!

Hoy es lunes.
¿Sabes tú los días de la semana?
lunes, martes, miércoles,
jueves, viernes, sábado y domingo.

Today is Monday.
Do you know the days of the week?
Monday, Tuesday, Wednesday,
Thursday, Friday, Saturday, Sunday.

LUNES
Monday

MARTES
Tuesday

MIÉRCOLES
Wednesday

JUEVES
Thursday

VIERNES
Friday

SÁBADO
Saturday

DOMINGO
Sunday

I eat breakfast.
I like bread and orange juice.

The weather is bad. It is raining.
I cannot go for a walk today.

Rain Medley

Rain, rain, go away
Come again another day
Rain, rain, go away
Little Johnny wants to play.

It's raining, it's pouring
The old man is snoring
He bumped his head and went to bed
And couldn't get up in the morning.

Está Lloviendo

Está lloviendo, está lloviendo
El viejo está roncando
Golpeó su cabeza y se fue
A la cama
No podía levantarse
En la mañana.

Arco Iris

A veces azul, a veces verde
Los colores más lindos
Que yo he visto
Rosado y lila, amarillo - ¡wii!
Me gusta sentarme en los arco iris.

Rainbows

Sometimes blue and sometimes green
Prettiest colors I've ever seen
Pink and purple, yellow - whee!
I love to ride those rainbows.

Aquí está mi escuela.
Yo digo,
"Buenos días, profesora."
Yo repito mis números
y mi alfabeto.

SCHOOL

mi escuela

Here is my school.
I say, "Good morning, teacher."
I repeat my numbers
and the alphabet.

Los Números

1 uno **2** dos **3** tres **4** cuatro **5** cinco **6** seis **7** siete **8** ocho **9** nueve **10** diez

Numbers
one   two   three   four   five   six   seven   eight   nine   ten

EL ALFABETO

A a (aah)   B b (beh)   C c (seh)   Ch (cheh)   D d (deh)   E e (eh)

F f (eh-feh)   G g (heh)   H h (ah-cheh)   I i (ee)   J j (hoh-tah)

K k (kah)   L l (eh-leh)   LL ll (eh-yeh)   M m (eh-meh)   N n (eh-neh)

Ñ ñ (eh-nyeh)   O o (oh)   P p (peh)   Q q (koo)   R r (eh-reh)

RR rr (err-reh)   S s (eh-seh)   T t (teh)   U u (oo)   V v (veh)

W w (doh-bleh-veh)   X x (eh-kees)   Y y (ee-gree-eh-gah)   Z z (seh-tah)

Ahora sé mi a-be-ce-da-ri-o.

Alphabet

A	B	C	Ch	D	E	F	G	H	I
J	K	L	LL	M	N	Ñ	O	P	Q
R	RR	S	T	U	V	W	X	Y	Z

Now I know my ABC's.

María Tenía un Borreguito

María tenía un borreguito, un borreguito, un borreguito
María tenía un borreguito, blanco como nieve
Un día la siguió a la escuela, a la escuela, a la escuela
Un día la siguió a la escuela, lo cual era prohibido.

Mary Had a Little Lamb

Mary had a little lamb, little lamb, little lamb
Mary had a little lamb, its fleece was white as snow
It followed her to school one day, school one day, school one day
It followed her to school one day, which was against the rules.

Un Elefante

Dos elefantes fueron a jugar
En una telaraña
Se alegraron tanto que
Llamaron a los otros elefantes a jugar.

Tres elefantes...
Cuatro elefantes...
Todos los elefantes...

One Elephant
One elephant went out to play
Upon a spider's web one day
He had such enormous fun
That he called for another elephant to come.

Two elephants...
Three elephants...
All elephants...

La Bamba

Para bailar la Bamba
Para bailar la Bamba
Se necesita una poca de gracia
Una poca de gracia y otra cosita.
¡Arriba!

La Bamba
To dance the bamba
To dance the bamba
A little grace is needed
A little grace plus a little bit of go.

La Cucaracha

La Cucaracha
La Cucaracha
Ya no puede caminar
Porque no tiene
Porque le falta
Patas para caminar.

La Cucaracha
La cucaracha, la cucaracha
Running up and down the wall
La cucaracha, la cucaracha
Me, I have no legs at all.

After school, we drive in our car to our house.

> Después de la escuela, nosotros manejamos el coche a la casa.

Las Ruedas del Coche

Las ruedas del coche van dando vueltas
Dando vueltas, dando vueltas
Las ruedas del coche van dando vueltas
Por todo el pueblo.

La bocina del coche suena pip pip pip
Pip pip pip, pip pip pip
La bocina del coche suena pip pip pip
Por todo el pueblo.

Los niños en el coche dicen
"Vamos a almorzar, vamos a almorzar
Vamos a almorzar"
Los niños en el coche dicen
"Vamos a almorzar"
Por todo el pueblo.

The Wheels on the Car

The wheels on the car go round and round
Round and round, round and round
The wheels on the car go round and round
All around the town.

The horn on the car goes beep beep beep
Beep beep beep, beep beep beep
The horn on the car goes beep beep beep
All around the town.

The children in the car go
"Let's have lunch, let's have lunch
Let's have lunch"
The children in the car go
"Let's have lunch"
All around the town.

Peter: Sister, what are we going to eat?
Marie: We are going to eat tortillas with beans.
Have some. Are they OK? I am going to try some.

Peter: Pass the salt.
Marie: Here. It is missing salt.

Peter: Thank you.
Marie: Do you want more beans?

Peter: No, thank you.
Marie: Mmm...The tortillas
are very good! Thanks, Mom!

It is time for lunch.
After lunch we take a nap.

Quieto Mi Niño
Quieto mi niño no llores
Tu papá te dará unas loras
Si esas loras no cantaran
Papá te comprará una oveja
Si la oveja no da buena lana
Entonces te dará una hermana
Si tu hermana no quiere jugar
Tu papá te llevará a un lindo lugar.

Hush Little Baby
Hush little baby don't say a word
Papa's going to buy you a mockingbird
If that mockingbird won't sing
Papa's going to buy you a diamond ring
If that diamond ring turns brass
Papa's going to buy you a looking glass
If that looking glass falls down
You'll still be the sweetest little baby in town.

Después de la siesta nosotros vamos al parque. Yo veo los patos. Yo canto "Me Gusta Ir a Pasear" con mis amigos.

After our naps, we go to the park. I see the ducks. I sing "I Love to Go a Wandering" with my friends.

Me Gusta Ir a Pasear
Me gusta ir a pasear por la senda del cerro
Me gusta ir a pasear con mi mochila puesta atrás
Valderré, valderrá, valderré, valderrá, ja-ja-ja
Valderré, valderrá
Con mi mochila puesta atrás.

I Love to Go a Wandering
I love to go a wandering along the mountain path
I love to go a wandering my knapsack on my back.
Valdore, valdora, valdore, valdora, ha-ha
Valdore, valdora
My knapsack on my back.

Jack y Jill

Jack y Jill subieron la cuesta
Para acarrear el agua
Jack se cayó
Quebró su corona
Y Jill se vino rodando.

Jack and Jill

Jack and Jill went up the hill
To fetch a pail of water
Jack fell down and broke his crown
And Jill came tumbling after.

Seis Patitos

Seis patitos que yo conocía
Gordos, flacos, bonitos también
Pero el patito
Con la pluma en su espalda
Guió a los otros con su
Cuac cuac cuac
Cuac cuac cuac
Cuac cuac cuac
Guió a los otros con su
Cuac cuac cuac.

Six Little Ducks

Six little ducks that I once knew
Fat ones, skinny ones, fair ones, too
But the one little duck
With the feather on his back
He led the others with his
Quack quack quack
Quack quack quack
Quack quack quack
He led the others with his
Quack quack quack.

Yo tengo hambre.
Es la hora de
la comida.

I am hungry.
It is time for dinner.

Oh! Susana

Yo vengo de Alabama
Mi banjo por mi rodilla
Me voy a Louisiana para ver a mi amor
Oh, Susana, no lloras para mí
Yo vengo de Alabama
Mi banjo por mi rodilla.

Oh! Susanna

Well, I come from Alabama
With a banjo on my knee
I'm goin' to Louisiana, my true love for to see
Oh, Susanna, won't you cry for me
'Cause I come from Alabama
With a banjo on my knee.

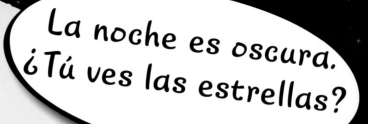

**La noche es oscura.
¿Tú ves las estrellas?**

The night is dark.
Do you see the stars?

Estrellita Brillarás

Estrellita brillarás
Todo lo iluminarás
Desde aquí yo te veré
Todo el cielo azul se ve
Estrellita brillarás
Todo lo iluminarás.

Twinkle, Twinkle
Twinkle, twinkle, little star
How I wonder what you are
Up above the world so high
Like a diamond in the sky
Twinkle, twinkle, little star
How I wonder what you are.

El Sereno

El sereno de mi calle
Tiene una voz muy bonita
Que cuando canta las horas
Parece una señorita
Sereno que canta, dime qué hora es
Que ha dado la una, las dos y las tres,
Las cuarto, las cinco, las seis, las siete,
Las ocho, las nueve, las diez.
Sereno que canta, dime qué hora es.

Night Watchman
The night watchman of my street
Has a very nice voice
When he sings the hours
He sounds like a woman
Night watchman who sings, tell me what time it is
He has announced one o'clock, two, three,
Four, five, six, seven, eight, nine, ten.
Night watchman who sings, tell me what time it is.

Buenas noches Mamá.
Buenas noches Papá.
Los quiero mucho.

Goodnight, Mommy.
Goodnight, Daddy.
I love you.

Buenas Noches Mis Amigos

Buenas noches mis amigos, buenas noches
Buenas noches mis amigos, buenas noches
Buenas noches, buenas noches
Buenas noches mis amigos, buenas noches.
¡Adios!

Goodnight My Friends
Goodnight, my friends, goodnight
Goodnight, my friends, goodnight
Goodnight, my friends
Goodnight, my friends
Goodnight, my friends, goodnight.
Goodnight!

¿Quieres aprender más?
(Want to learn more?)

la lámpara

el banjo

el sillón

la pelota

el perro

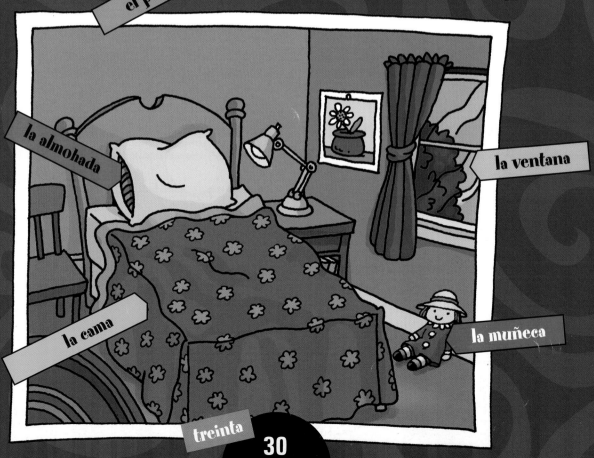

la almohada

la ventana

la cama

la muñeca

el chocolate caliente

el jugo de naranja

el pan

la mermelada

el árbol

la amiga

el puente

la pelota de soccer

los colores

rojo

azul

morado

vierde

anaranjado

gris

amarillo

rosado

marrón

blanco

negro